The Church is the people of God.

THE BIBLE SAYS IN 1 PETER 2:9-10,

"But you are a chosen race, a royal priesthood, a holy nation, a people for his possession, so that you may proclaim the praises of the one who called you out of darkness into his marvelous light. Once you were not a people, but now you are God's people; you had not received mercy, but now you have received mercy."

As the church, we are God's people.
He has set us apart as His own.

We have our own church family that we meet with often to worship God, and then we have the global church family that is spread out across the world. We may never meet some of these believers on earth, but we know that God has built us together and that we are His church.

God promised to help us be His church.

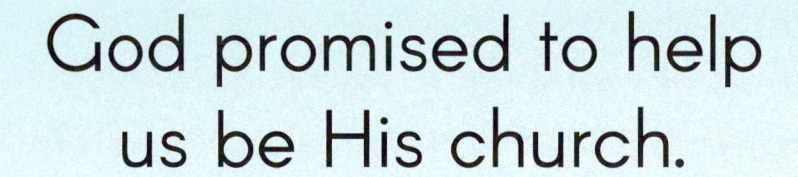

JESUS SAYS IN JOHN 14:15,

"If you love me, you will keep my commands. And I will ask the Father, and he will give you another Counselor to be with you forever. He is the Spirit of truth. The world is unable to receive him because it doesn't see him or know him. But you do know him, because he remains with you and will be in you."

Jesus tells us that we show our love for Him by keeping His commands. Do you know how hard it is for us to keep His commands? Sometimes it's easier for us to be selfish than sharing, or unkind than loving. It seems pretty hard to keep God's commands.

But Jesus promised to send us a Counselor who would help us to keep God's commands. He promised to send the Holy Spirit to believers, and now the Holy Spirit guides us and helps us keep Jesus' commands and helps us to show God that we love Him.

God sent His Spirit to the church.

ACTS 2:42 TELLS US,

"They devoted themselves to the apostles' teaching, to the fellowship, to the breaking of bread, and to prayer."

Acts 2 shows us that God kept His promise to send a Helper.

Through the Spirit each Christian has a Counselor to help them love God the way He deserves to be loved. God kept His promise, and now we have help to flee from sin through the Holy Spirit!

Now, we follow the example that the church in Acts gives us. We learn about God through the Bible. We eat and fellowship. We pray together. This is God's plan for the Church.

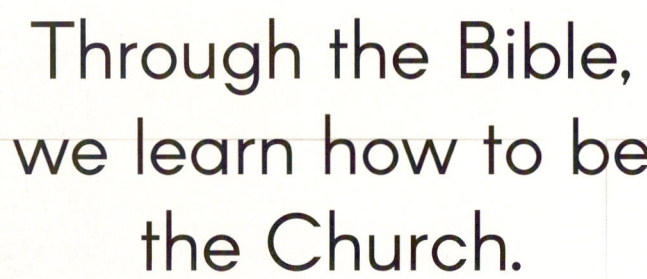

Through the Bible, we learn how to be the Church.

IN COLOSSIANS 3:16 WE ARE TOLD

"Let the word of Christ dwell richly among you, in all wisdom teaching and admonishing one another through psalms, hymns, and spiritual songs, singing to God with gratitude in your hearts."

When we meet with the church, we learn about God from His Word.

Through our Bibles, we are able to encourage one another with the truth about who God is and what He has done for us.

When we meet with God's people, we sing songs about what we know about God, praising Him for His goodness. Meeting with the church grows us in thankfulness.

The Church calls us in obedience to God's Word.

JAMES 1:22 TELLS US,

"But be doers of the word and not hearers only, deceiving yourselves."

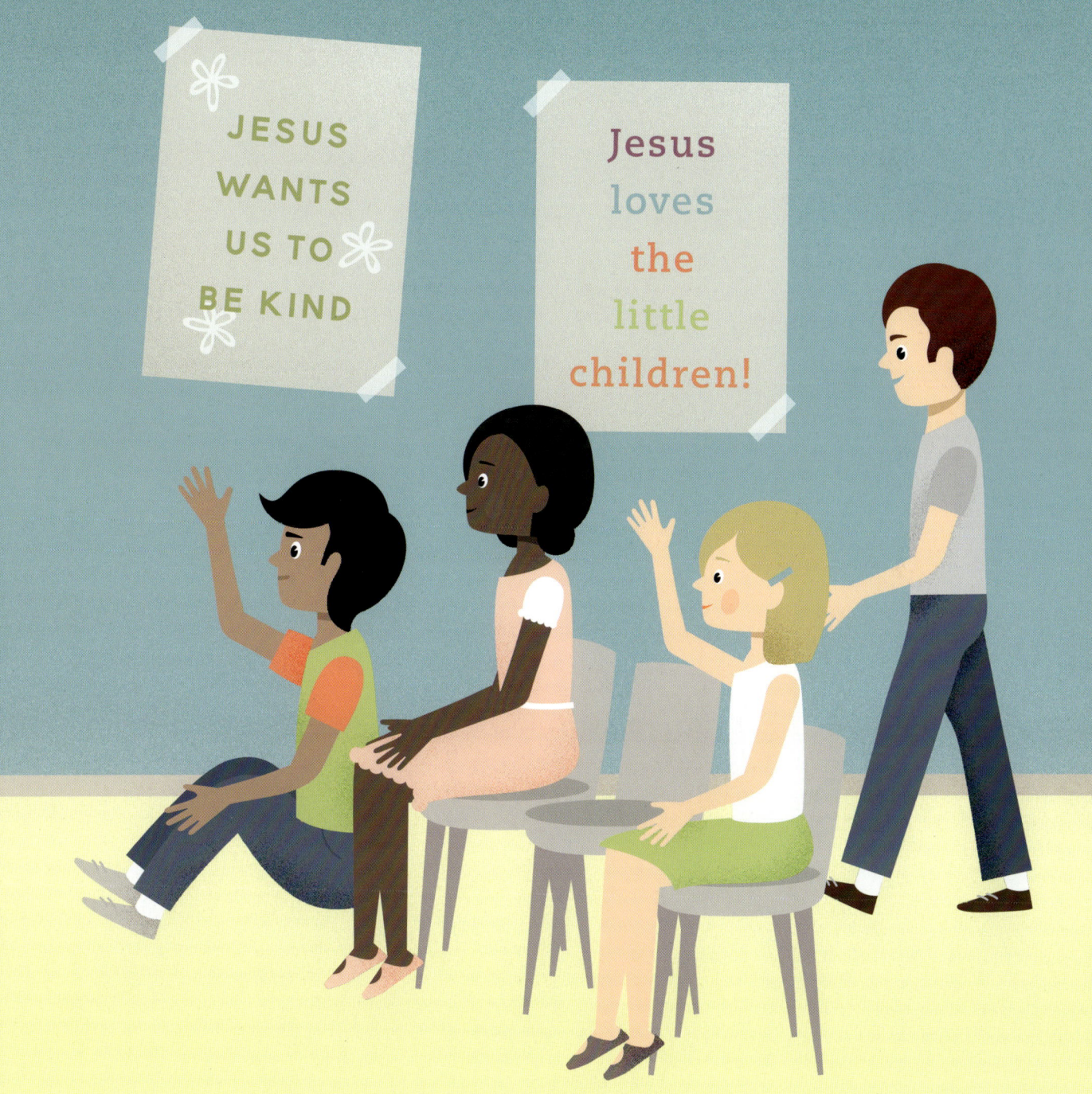

When we learn about God's Word, we are taught how we should live. We must obey what God says to us through our Bibles. When we are a part of a church, our church family helps us to live in a way that honors God.

God wants us to meet together as a Church.

IN HEBREWS 10:24-25 WE READ

"And let us watch out for one another to provoke love and good works, not neglecting to gather together, as some are in the habit of doing, but encouraging each other, and all the more as you see the day approaching."

The job for the church now is to meet together with our heavenly family often so that we can encourage and love one another.

When we go to church, we get to meet with other Christians, growing closer as a family.

God gives us leaders.

HEBREWS 13:17 TELLS US,

"Obey your leaders and submit to them, since they keep watch over your souls as those who will give an account, so that they can do this with joy and not with grief, for that would be unprofitable for you."

Within the church God gives us leaders and authorities for us to follow.

These pastors and teachers watch over us and are responsible for us to God. We should respect and pray for our leaders, knowing that they want us to grow in our relationship with God and with others in our church family.

 Who are the different leaders in your church? How can you pray for them?

God gives us gifts to serve the church with.

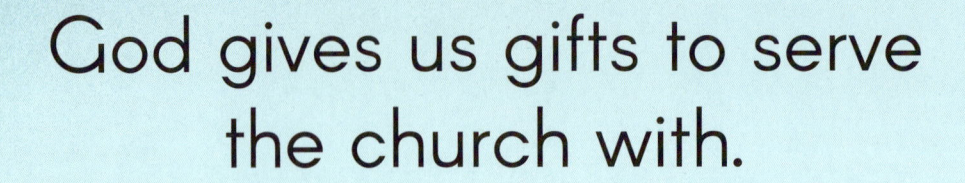

WE READ IN 1 CORINTHIANS 12:12,

"For just as the body is one and has many parts, and all the parts of that body, though many, are one body — so also is Christ."

In His Church, God has given everyone gifts.

All of these gifts look different, but they have the same purpose: to serve God and the church. Through our gifts, God gives us opportunity to build up and encourage His church so that we can work like a body—lots of small parts working together for one big purpose.

 What gifts has God given to you? How can you use your talents and skills to serve in your church?

Now, we invite others to be a part of the Church.

WE ARE COMMANDED IN MATTHEW 28:19-20,

"Go, therefore, and make disciples of all nations, baptizing them in the name of the Father and of the Son and of the Holy Spirit, teaching them to observe everything I have commanded you. And remember, I am with you always, to the end of the age."